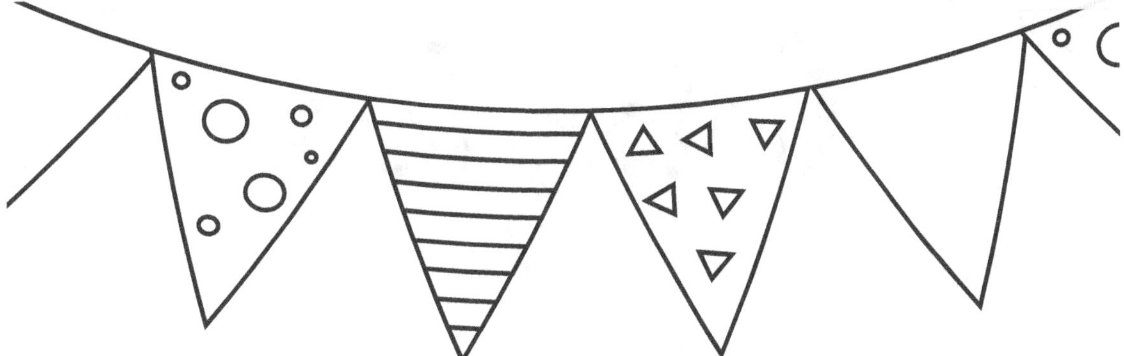

# This Book Belongs T

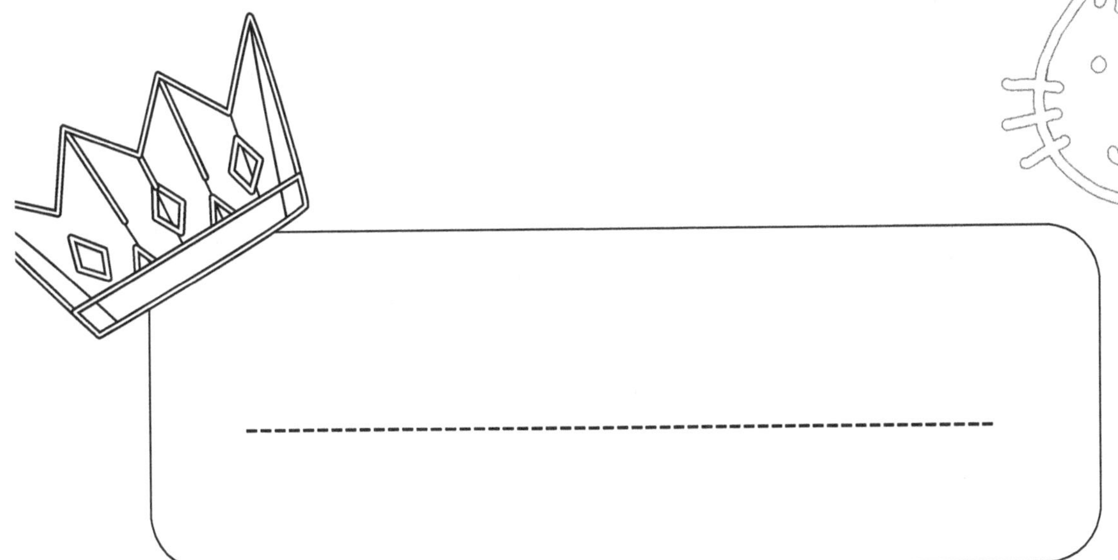

# Color Test

Mag
Unicat

GOOD
Night

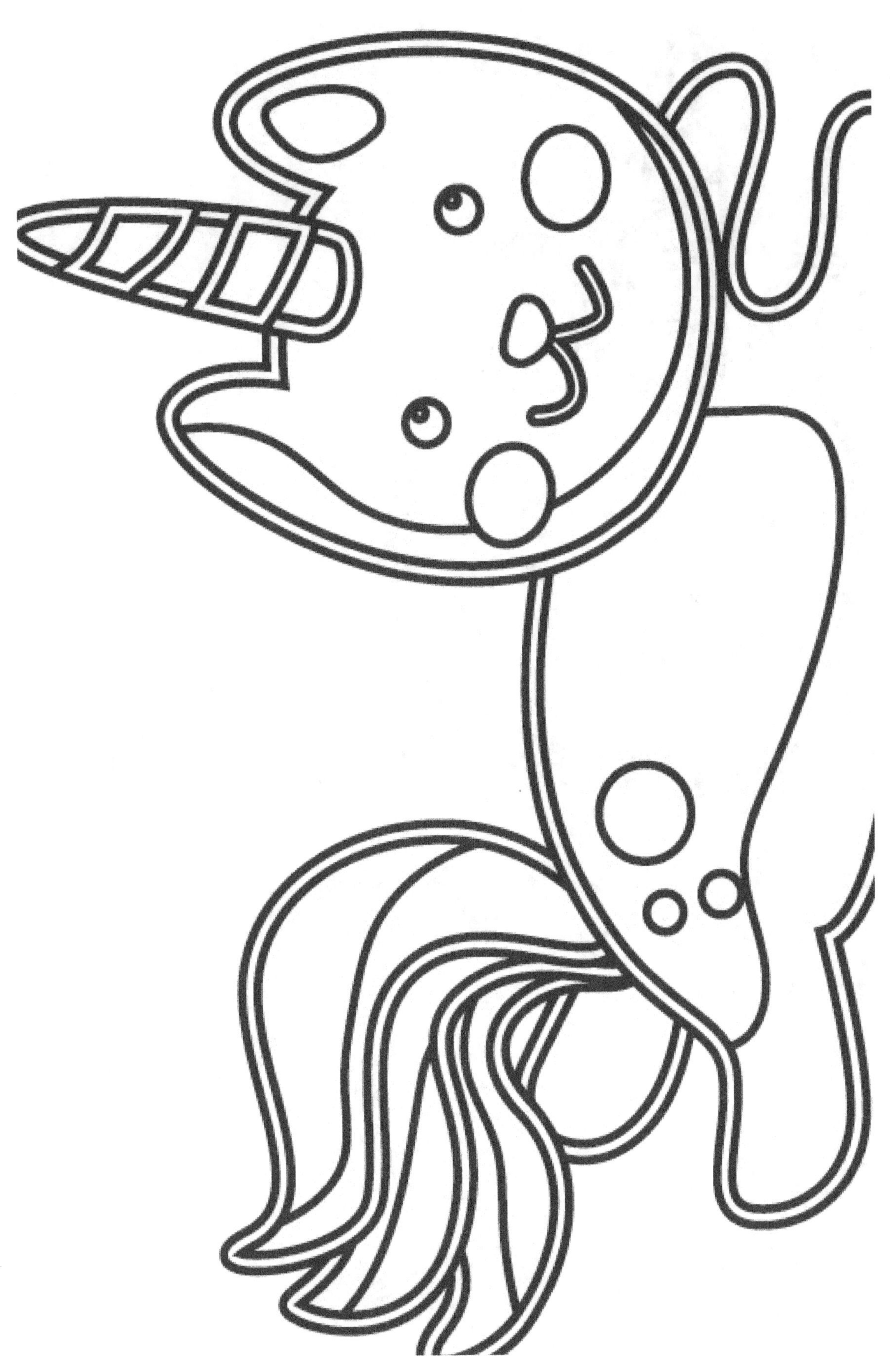

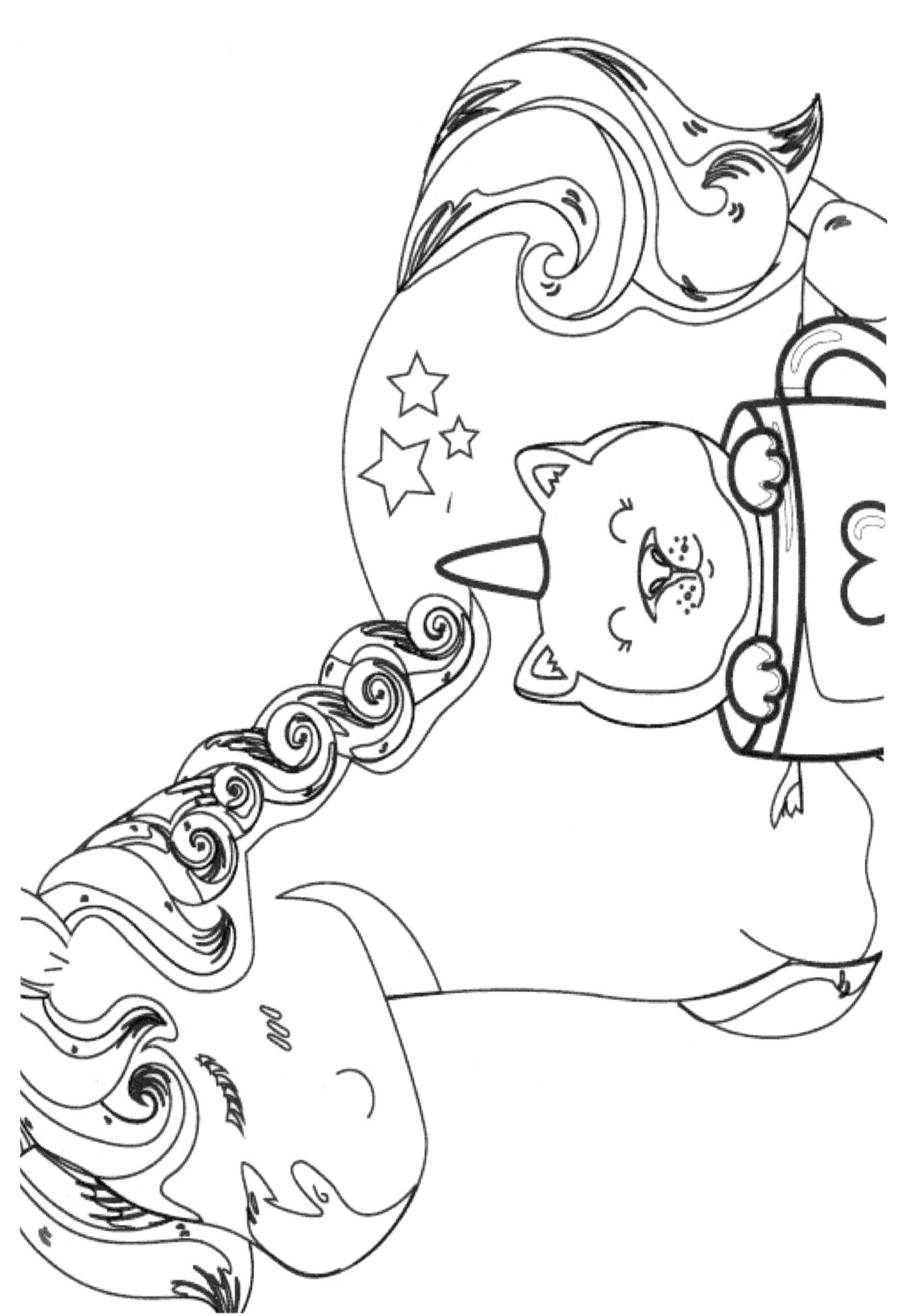

meowgical

UNICOR
is a
CAT

rick
gr
reat

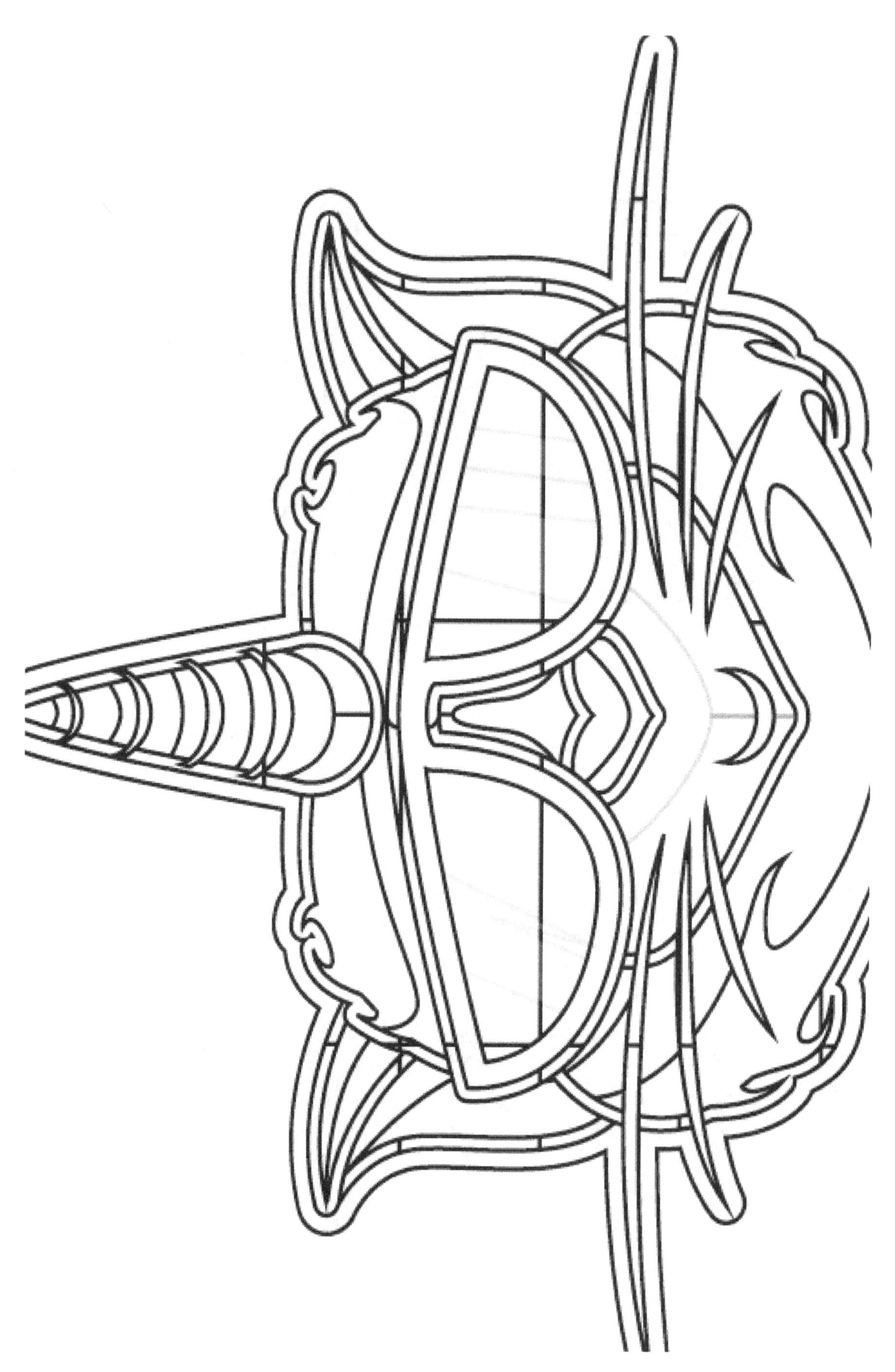

MEOW

HELLO!
Ooops!

oops!

Ooops!
ello!

Hello

Hello!

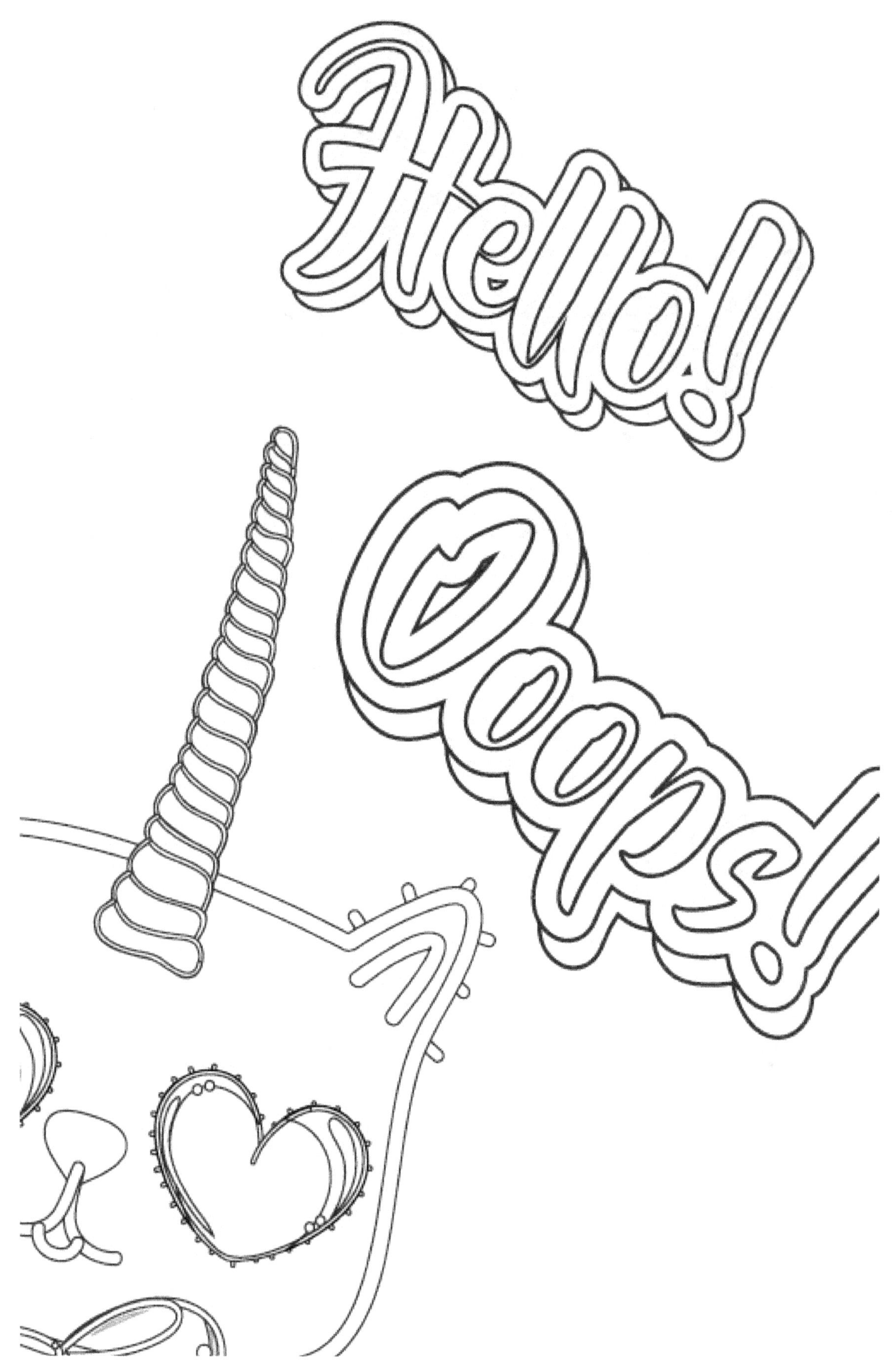

Hello!
Oops!

Hello

Hello

Hello

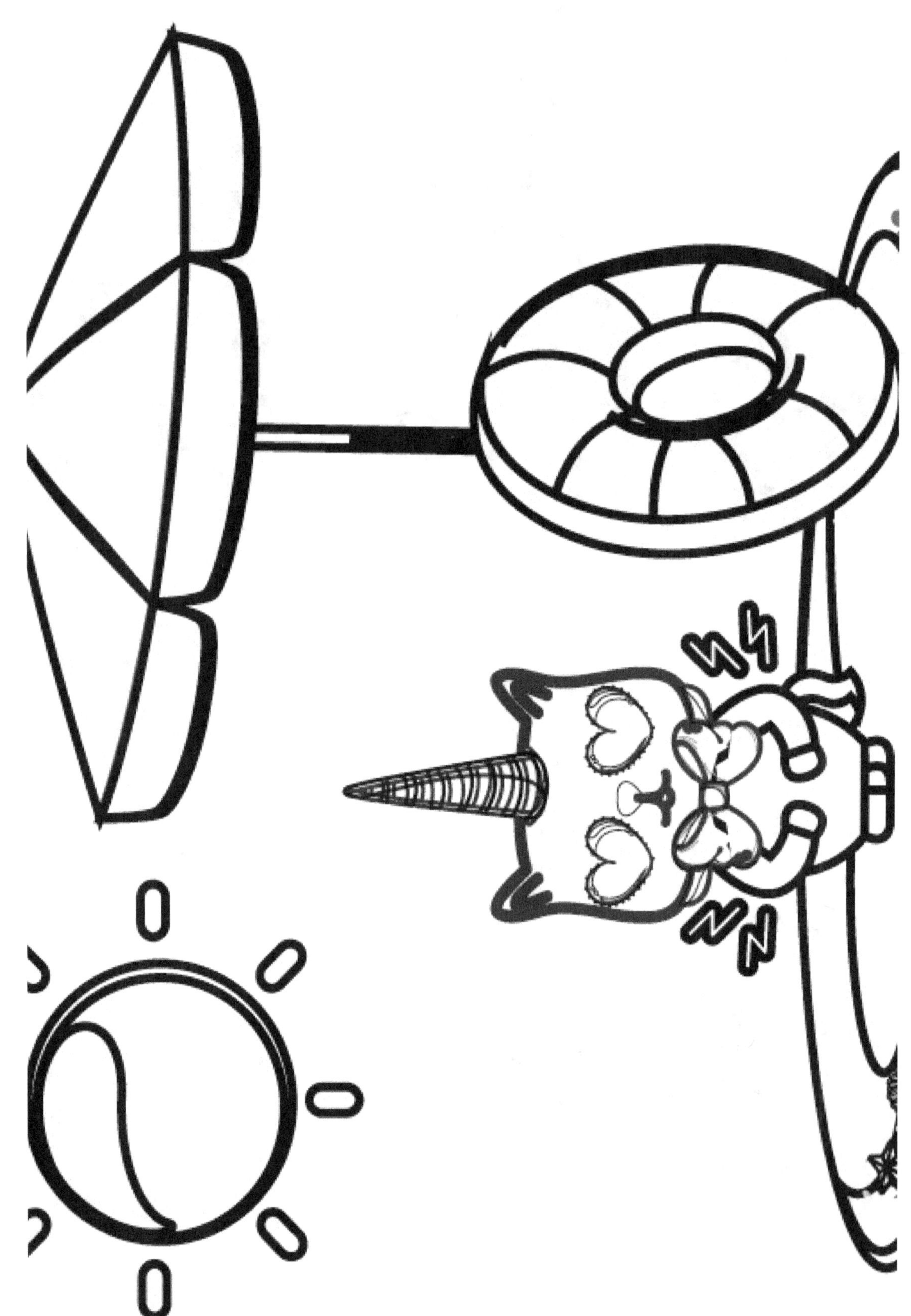

ZZZ

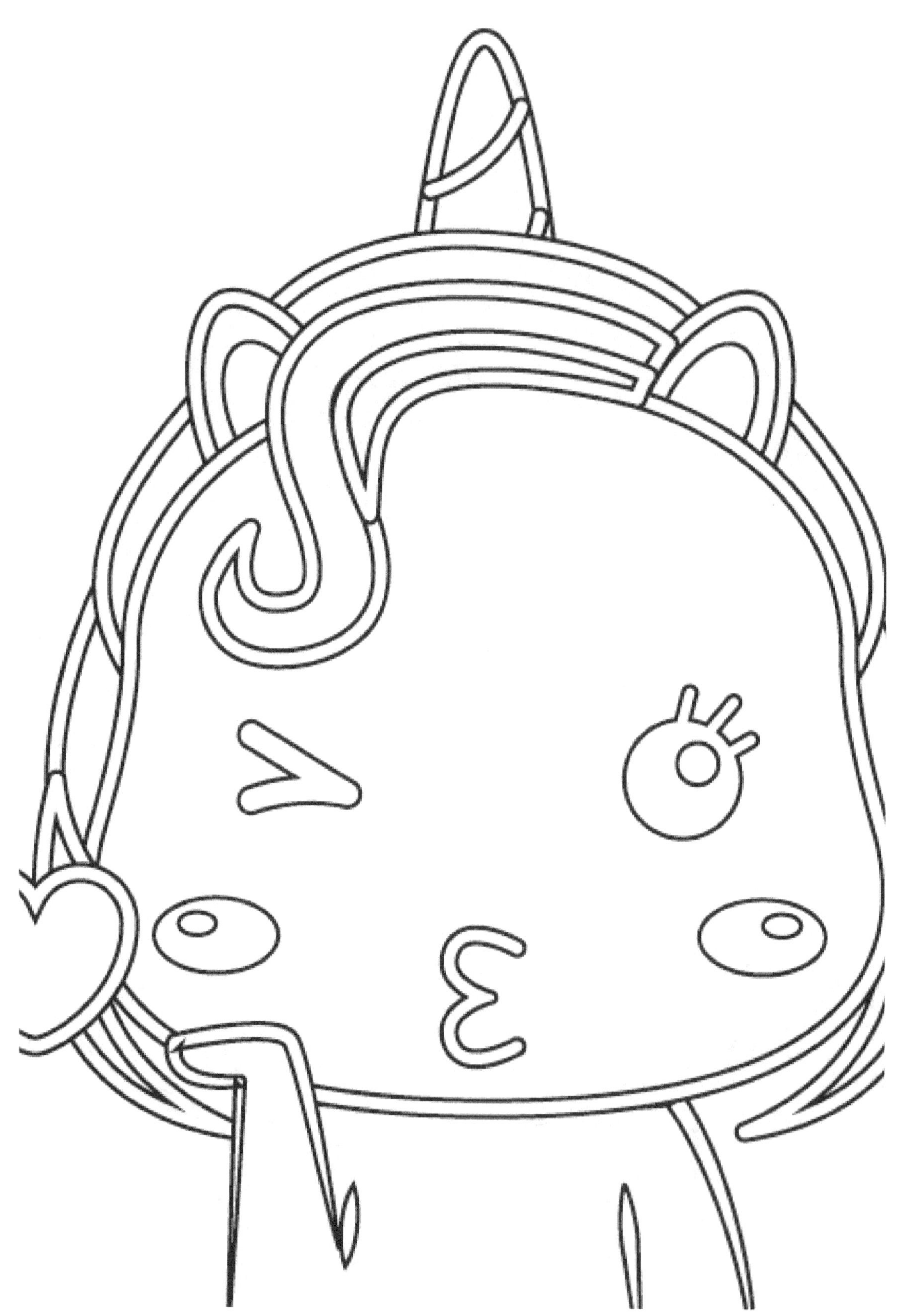

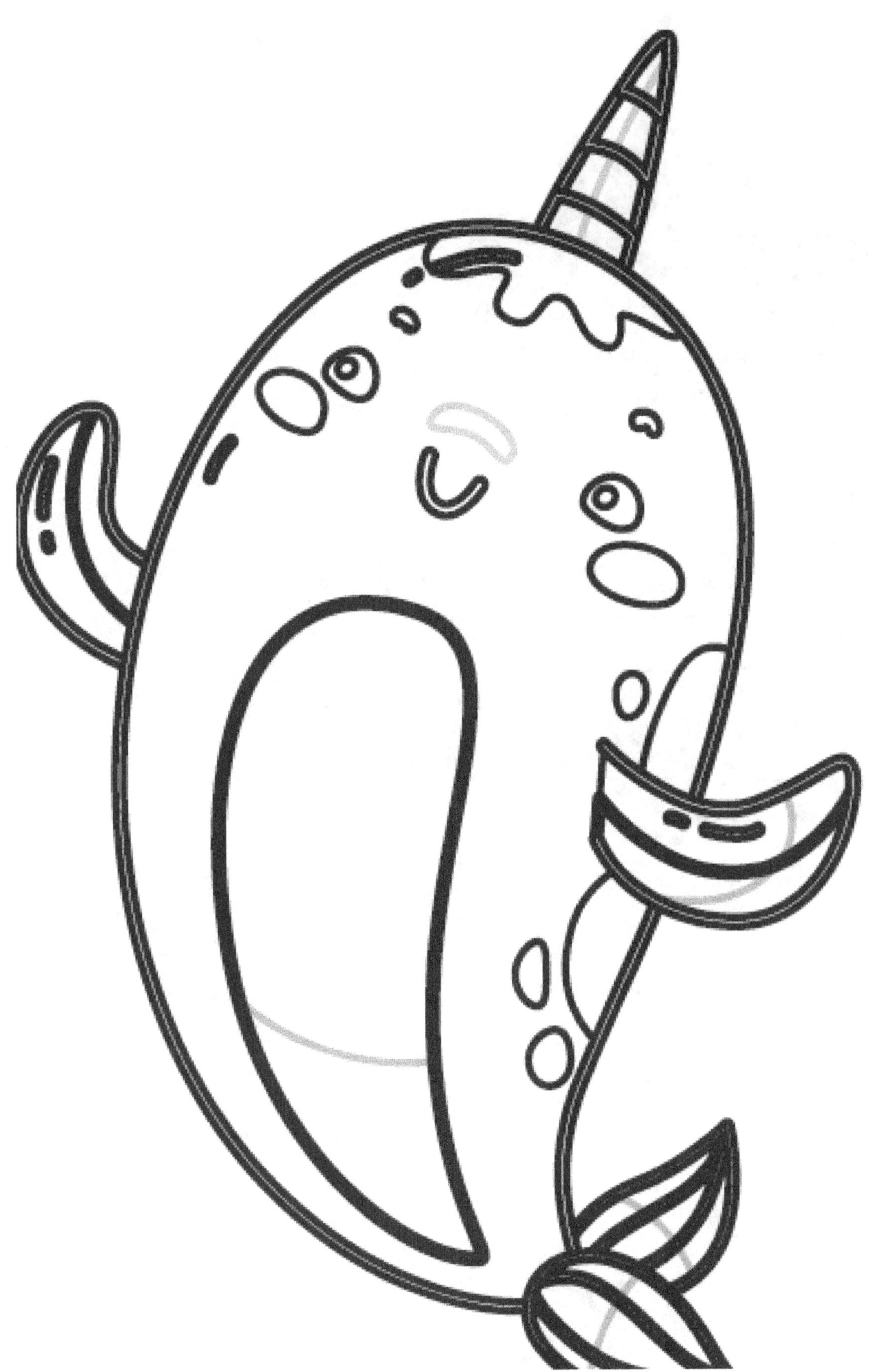

Thank you for being our valued customer.

We are so grateful for the pleasure serving you  and hope we met your expectations.

ake sure you have the best experience using this coloring bc
o prevent bleeding, although the illustrations are on one-sic
commend coloring using pencils.

are going to use any kind of ink that may cause bleeding
ghout the pages, we recommend tearing out the coloring
 or using a buffer page.